TAMIL VOWEL CONSONANTS FOR TODDLERS

TAMIL UNLIMITED LLC
10 Maybelle Court, Mechanicsburg PA 17050
tamilanitham.com

Title	*:Tamil Vowel Consonants For Toddlers*
ISBN	*:979-8-9909905-1-7*
Subject	*:Juvenile nonfiction*
Language	*:Tamil,English*
Edition	*:Print 2025*
Book Size	*:8.000" x 8.000" (203mm x 203mm)*
Font	*:Tamil Virtual AcademyTAU Marutham,TAMUni-Tamil046*
Printing	*: IngramSpark*
Publication	*:TAMIL UNLIMITED LLC* *10 Maybelle Court, Mechanicsburg, PA,17050, USA.* *+17178025889 ,+17177283999* *tamilunltd@gmail.com*

Pronunciation Guide

Vowels:

There are five basic vowel sounds in Tamilஅ(/ă/), இ(/ĭ/), உ(/ŏŏ/), எ(/ĕ/), ஒ(/ŏ/). These sounds can be short and long. Short and long vowels have distinct forms to denote their pronunciation length. There are five short vowels and seven long vowels. When vowels take one second to pronounce, they are short vowels. A letter with one underline means it is a short sound. When vowels take two seconds to pronounce, they are long vowels. The letter with double underlines means it is a longer sound. Tamil vowels have two diphthongs. ஐ(/aɪ/) and ஔ (/aw/). அ(/ă/)and இ(/ĭ/) vowel sounds are within the ஐ(/aɪ/) syllable. அ(/ă/) and உ (/ŏŏ/) vowel sounds are with in the ஔ syllable. These two diphthongs are also long vowels.

அ ஆ

Consonants:

There are eighteen consonants in Tamil. Tamil Consonants have a circle or a dot above them. Consonants take half a second to pronounce. The consonants are pronounced in three distinct ways, depending upon where the sound begins. Their pronunciation originates from the chest, throat, or nose.

The hard tone letters:

The hard sounding letters start from the chest with pressure. The thick lines indicate hardness.

க ச் ட் த் ப் ற்

The soft tone letters:

Soft-sounding letters are nasal sounds with minimal pressure and effort. The wavy lines indicate softness.

ங் ஞ் ண் ந் ம் ன்

The mid tone letters:

Letters with in-between sounds initiate from the throat, which is between the chest and nose, so they are referred to as "in-between letters". The dotted lines indicate the mid sound characteristics.

ய் ர் ல் வ் ழ் ள்

The Vowel_consonants:

When vowels are added to these consonants, they get their own form and sound. These letters are called vowel-consonant letters. Because of their association with vowels, the vowel-consonant letters also have either short or long pronunciation durations. The short pronunciations are indicated by an underline, and the long pronunciations are indicated by a double underline. The consonants and the vowel-consonants get their names based on where their initial sound begins.

அ

(/ă/),(/ŭ/),(/æ/),(/ʌ/)

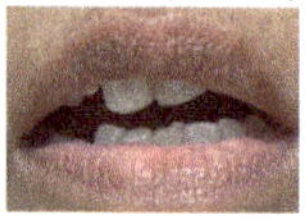

ஆ

(/ŏ/),(/ɒ/)

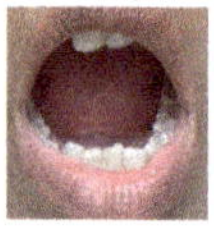

இ

(/ĭ/),(/ɪ/)

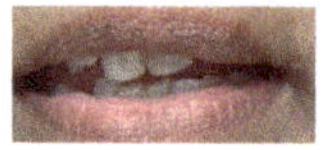

ஈ

(/ē/),(/i:/)

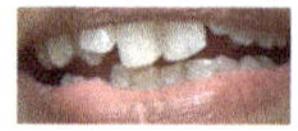

உ

(/ŏŏ/),(/ʊ/)

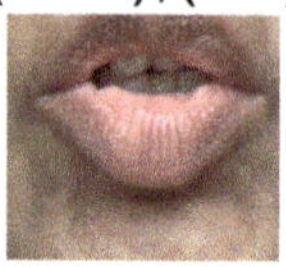

ஊ

(/u/),(/u:/)

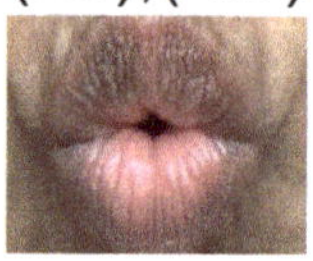

எ

(/ĕ/),(/e/)

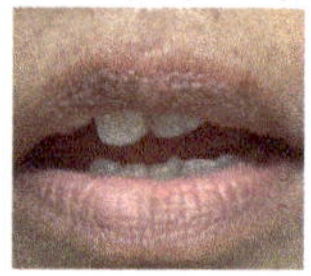

ஏ

(/ā/), (/eɪ/)

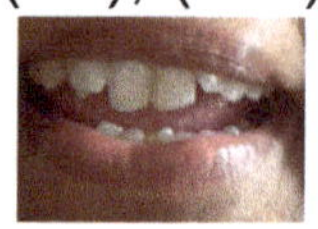

ஐ

/aɪ/

ஒ

(/ŏ/),(/ɔ:/)

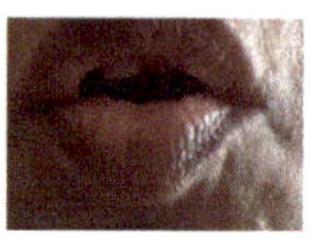

ஓ

(/ō/), (/ow/),(/oʊ/)

ஔ

(/aw/),(/ou/),(/oʊ/)

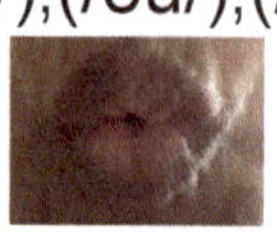

க்
/k/
Say ik as in kite

ங்
/ŋ/
Say ing as in song

ச்
/tʃ/
Say ich as in march

ஞ்
/ɲ/
Say inj as in banjo

ட்
/t/
Say it as in time

ண்
/n/
Say in as in tan

த்
/t̪/
Say ith as in thin

ந்
/n̪/
Say inth as in month

ப்
/p/
Say ip as in pan

ம்
/m/
Say im as in man

ய்
/j/
Say iy as in you

ர்
/r/
Say ir as in run

ல்
/l̪/
Say il as in level

வ்
/ʋ/
Say iv as in van

ழ்
/ɹ̣/
Say izhl as in cycle

ள்
/ɭ/
Say ll as in black

ற்
/ɹ/,[r͡r]
Say ır as ın red

ன்
/n/
Say in as in fun

மூக்கு
mookku

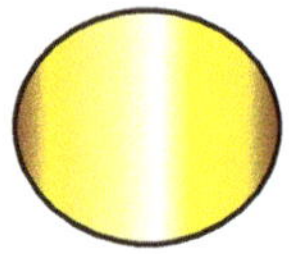

தங்கம்
thanggam

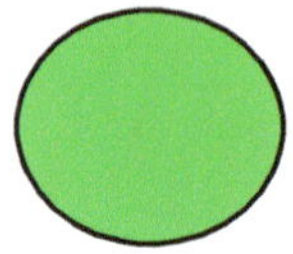

பச்சை
pachchai

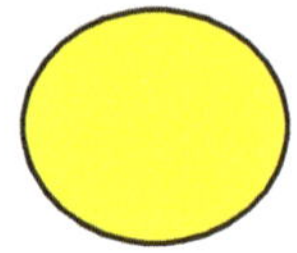

மஞ்சள்
manjjaLl

8
எட்டு
ehttu

2
இரண்டு
earanndu

10
பத்து
paththu

5
ஐந்து
ainththu

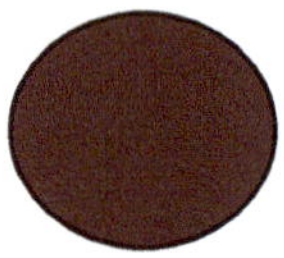

பழுப்பு
pazhLooppu

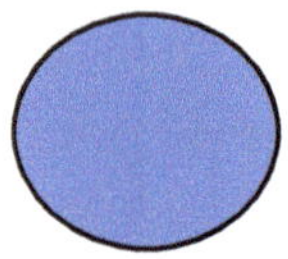

நீலம்
neelam

வாய்
vaai

நீர்
neer

கால்
kaal

செவ்வகம்
sevhvakam

இதழ்
eathazhL

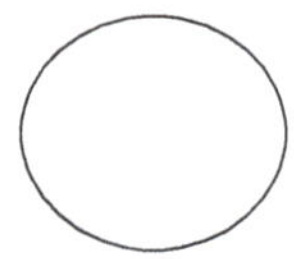

வெள்ளை
veLlLlai

நாற்காலி
naaRrkaali

9
ஒன்பது
ohnbathu

அ+க்=க a+ik=ka	ஆ+க்=கா aw+ik=kaa
இ+க்=கி ea+ik=ki	ஈ+க்=கீ ee+ik=kee
உ+க்=கு wu+ik=ku	ஊ+க்=கூ oo+ik=koo
எ+க்=கெ eh+ik=keh	ஏ+க்=கே ay+ik=kay
ஐ+க்=கை ai+ik=kai	
ஒ+க்=கொ oh+ik=koh	ஓ+க்=கோ ohh+ik=kohh
ஔ+க்=கௌ ow+ik=kow	

அ+ங்=ங a+ing=nga	ஆ+ங்=ஙா aw+ing=ngaa
இ+ங்=ஙி ea+ing=ngi	ஈ+ங்=ஙீ ee+ing=ngee
உ+ங்=ஙு wu+ing=ngu	ஊ+ங்=ஙூ oo+ing=ngoo
எ+ங்=ஙெ eh+ing=ngeh	ஏ+ங்=ஙே ay+ing=ngay
ஐ+ங்=ஙை ai+ing=ngai	
ஒ+ங்=ஙொ oh+ing=ngoh	ஓ+ங்=ஙோ ohh+ing=ngohh
ஔ+ங்=ஙௌ ow+ing=ngow	

அ+ச்=ச a+ich=cha	ஆ+ச்=சா aw+ich=chaa
இ+ச்=சி ea+ich=chi	ஈ+ச்=சீ ee+ich=chee
உ+ச்=சு wu+ich=chu	ஊ+ச்=சூ oo+ich=choo
எ+ச்=செ eh+ich=cheh	ஏ+ச்=சே ay+ich=chay
ஐ+ச்=சை ai+ich=chai	
ஒ+க்=கொ oh+ich=choh	ஓ+ச்=சோ ohh+ich=chohh
ஔ+ச்=சௌ ow+ich=chow	

a+inj=nja அ+ஞ்=ஞ	aw+inj=njaa ஆ+ஞ்=ஞா
ea+inj=nji இ+ஞ்=ஞி	ee+inj=njee ஈ+ஞ்=ஞீ
wu+inj=nju உ+ஞ்=ஞு	oo+inj=njoo ஊ+ஞ்=ஞூ
eh+inj=njeh எ+ஞ்=ஞெ	ay+inj=njay ஏ+ஞ்=ஞே

ai+inj=njai

ஐ+ஞ்=ஞை

oh+inj=njoh ஒ+ஞ்=ஞொ	ohh+inj=njohh ஓ+ஞ்=ஞோ

ow+inj=njow

ஔ+ஞ்=ஞௌ

அ+ட்=ட a+it=ta	ஆ+ட்=டா aw+it=taa
இ+ட்=டி ea+it=ti	ஈ+ட்=டீ ee+it=tee
உ+ட்=டு wu+it=tu	ஊ+ட்=டூ oo+it=too
எ+ட்=டெ eh+it=teh	ஏ+ட்=டே ay+it=tay
ஐ+ட்=டை ai+it=tai	
ஒ+ட்=டொ oh+it=toh	ஓ+ட்=டோ ohh+it=tohh
ஔ+ட்=டௌ ow+it=tow	

அ + ண் = ண a+iN=Na	ஆ + ண் = ணா aw+iN=Naa
இ + ண் = ணி ea+iN=Ni	ஈ + ண் = ணீ ee+iN=Nee
உ + ண் = ணு wu+iN=Nu	ஊ + ண் = ணூ oo+iN=Noo
எ + ண் = ணெ eh+iN=Neh	ஏ + ண் = ணே ay+iN=Nay
ஐ + ண் = ணை ai+iN=Nai	
ஒ + ண் = ணொ oh+iN=Noh	ஓ + ண் = ணோ ohh+iN=Nohh
ஔ + ண் = ணௌ ow+iN=Now	

அ+த்=த	a+ith=tha	ஆ+த்=தா	aw+ith=thaa
இ+த்=தி	ea+ith=thi	ஈ+த்=தீ	ee+ith=thee
உ+த்=தி	wu+ith=thu	ஊ+த்=து	oo+ith=thoo
எ+த்=தி	eh+ith=theh	ஏ+த்=தே	ay+ith=thay
ஐ+த்=தை	ai+ith=thai		
ஒ+த்=தொ	oh+ith=thoh	ஓ+த்=தோ	ohh+ith=thohh
ஔ+த்=தௌ	ow+ith=thow		

a+inth=na அ+ந்=ந	aw+inth=naa ஆ+ந்=நா
ea+inth=ni இ+ந்=நி	ee+inth=nee ஈ+ந்=நீ
wu+inth=nu உ+ந்=நு	oo+inth=noo ஊ+ந்=நூ
eh+inth=neh எ+ந்=நெ	ay+inth=nay ஏ+ந்=நே
ai+inth=nai ஐ+ந்=நை	
oh+inth=noh ஒ+ந்=நொ	ohh+inth=nohh ஓ+ந்=நோ
ow+inth=now ஔ+ந்=நௌ	

அ+ப்=ப a+ip=pa	ஆ+ப்=பா aw+ip=paa
இ+ப்=பி ea+ip=pi	ஈ+ப்=பீ ee+ip=pee
உ+ப்=பு wu+ip=pu	ஊ+ப்=பூ oo+ip=poo
எ+ப்=பெ eh+ip=peh	ஏ+ப்=பே ay+ip=pay
ஐ+ப்=பை ai+ip=pai	
ஒ+ப்=பொ oh+ip=poh	ஓ+ப்=போ ohh+ip=pohh
ஔ+ப்=பௌ ow+ip=pow	

a+im=ma அ+ம்=ம	aw+im=maa ஆ+ம்=மா
ea+im=mi இ+ம்=மி	ee+im=mee ஈ+ம்=மீ
wu+im=mu உ+ம்=மு	oo+im=moo ஊ+ம்=மூ
eh+im=meh எ+ம்=மெ	ay+im=may ஏ+ம்=மே
ai+im=mai ஐ+ம்=மை	
oh+im=moh ஒ+ம்=மொ	ohh+im=mohh ஓ+ம்=மோ
ow+im=mow ஔ+ம்=மௌ	

அ+ய்=ய a+iy=ya	ஆ+ய்=யா aw+iy=yaa
இ+ய்=யி ea+iy=yi	ஈ+ய்=யீ ee+iy=yee
உ+ய்=யு wu+iy=yu	ஊ+ய்=யூ oo+iy=yoo
எ+ய்=யெ eh+iy=yeh	ஏ+ய்=யே ay+iy=yay
ஐ+ய்=யை ai+iy=yai	
ஒ+ய்=யொ oh+iy=yoh	ஓ+ய்=யோ ohh+iy=yohh
ஔ+ய்=யௌ ow+iy=yow	

அ+ர்=ர	a+ir=ra	ஆ+ர்=ரா	aw+ir=raa
இ+ர்=ரி	ea+ir=ri	ஈ+ர்=ரீ	ee+ir=ree
உ+ர்=ரு	wu+ir=ru	ஊ+ர்=ரூ	oo+ir=roo
எ+ர்=ரெ	eh+ir=reh	ஏ+ய்=ரே	ay+ir=ray
ஐ+ர்=ரை	ai+ir=rai		
ஒ+ர்=ரொ	oh+ir=roh	ஓ+ர்=ரோ	ohh+ir=rohh
ஔ+ர்=ரௌ	ow+ir=row		

அ+ல்=ல (a+il=la)	ஆ+ல்=லா (aw+il=laa)
இ+ல்=லி (ea+il=li)	ஈ+ல்=லீ (ee+il=lee)
உ+ல்=லு (wu+il=lu)	ஊ+ல்=லூ (oo+il=loo)
எ+ல்=லெ (eh+il=leh)	ஏ+ல்=லே (ay+il=lay)

ai+il=lai

ஐ+ல்=லை

ஒ+ல்=லொ (oh+il=loh)	ஓ+ல்=லோ (ohh+il=lohh)

ow+il=low

ஔ+ல்=லௌ

அ+வ்=வ a+iy=ya	ஆ+வ்=வா aw+iy=yaa
இ+வ்=வி ea+iy=yi	ஈ+வ்=வீ ee+iy=yee
உ+வ்=வு wu+iy=yu	ஊ+வ்=வூ oo+iy=yoo
எ+வ்=வெ eh+iy=yeh	ஏ+வ்=வே ay+iy=yay
ஐ+வ்=வை ai+iy=yai	
ஒ+வ்=வொ oh+iy=yoh	ஓ+வ்=வோ ohh+iy=yohh
ஔ+வ்=வௌ ow+iy=yow	

a+izhl=zhla அ+ழ்=ழ	aw+izhl=zhlaa ஆ+ழ்=ழா
ea+izhl=zhli இ+ழ்=ழி	ee+izhl=zhlee ஈ+ழ்=ழீ
wu+izhl=zhlu உ+ழ்=ழு	oo+izhl=zhloo ஊ+ழ்=ழூ
eh+izhl=zhleh எ+ழ்=ழெ	ay+izhl=zhlay ஏ+ழ்=ழே
ai+izhl=zhlai ஐ+ழ்=ழை	
oh+izhl=zhloh ஒ+ழ்=ழொ	ohh+izhl=zhlohh ஓ+ழ்=ழோ
ow+izhl=zhlow ஔ+ழ்=ழௌ	

அ+ள்=ள a+iLL=LLa	ஆ+ள்=ளா aw+iLL=LLaa
இ+ள்=ளி ea+iLL=LLi	ஈ+ள்=ளீ ee+iLL=LLee
உ+ள்=ளு wu+iLL=LLu	ஊ+ள்=ளூ oo+iLL=LLoo
எ+ள்=ளெ eh+iLL=LLeh	ஏ+ள்=ளே ay+iLL=LLay
ஐ+ள்=ளை ai+iLL=LLai	
ஒ+ள்=ளொ oh+iLL=LLoh	ஓ+ள்=ளோ ohh+iLL=LLohh
ஔ+ள்=ளௌ ow+iLL=LLow	

அ+ற்=ற a+irr=rra	ஆ+ற்=றா aw+irr=rraa
இ+ற்=றி ea+irr=rri	ஈ+ற்=றீ ee+irr=rree
உ+ற்=று wu+irr=rru	ஊ+ற்=றூ oo+irr=rroo
எ+ற்=றெ eh+irr=rreh	ஏ+ற்=றே ay+irr=rray
ஐ+ற்=றை ai+irr=rrai	
ஒ+ற்=றொ oh+irr=rroh	ஓ+ற்=றோ ohh+irr=rrohh
ஔ+ற்=றௌ ow+irr=rrow	

அ+ன்=ன (a+n=na)	ஆ+ன்=னா (aw+n=naa)
இ+ன்=னி (ea+n=n)	ஈ+ன்=னீ (ee+n=nee)
உ+ன்=னு (wu+n=nu)	ஊ+ன்=னூ (oo+n=noo)
எ+ன்=னெ (eh+n=neh)	ஏ+ன்=னே (ay+n=nay)
ஐ+ன்=னை (a+n=na)	
ஒ+ன்=னொ (oh+n=noh)	ஓ+ன்=னோ (ohh+n=nohh)
ஔ+ன்=னௌ (ow+n=now)	

www.ingramcontent.com/pod-product-compliance
Lightning Source LLC
LaVergne TN
LVHW070046061026
849530LV00009B/81
9798990990517